THE OFFICIAL
ANNUAL 2024

WRITTEN BY STEVE BARTRAM
DESIGNED BY DANIEL JAMES

A Grange Publication

©2023. Published by Grange Communications Ltd., Edinburgh, under
licence from Manchester United Football Club. Printed in the EU.

Photography © MUFC.

ISBN : 978-1-915879-25-7

CONTENTS

WELCOME TO THE 2024 MANCHESTER UNITED ANNUAL!

This year's edition of your favourite United book features profiles of some of your most loved players in the men's and women's first teams, plus the two men in charge of the sides: Erik ten Hag and Marc Skinner.

We also delve into some big numbers: looking at Marcus Rashford's sensational 2022/23 scoring season and his place in the Reds' all-time scoring charts; running through the history of United's Premier League squad numbers and delving into the club's Champions League record.

On a personal level, we also get to know more about players' interests away from football and gain insight into the dressing room tunes enjoyed on matchday. Speaking of music, we also have an exclusive interview with singer, top Red – and top midfielder – Tom Grennan!

There's all of this and more besides in the 2024 Manchester United Annual. As ever, your knowledge of the Reds will be tested with our in-depth quiz section, and you'll have the chance to enter our competition to win a signed United shirt.

Enjoy reading!

MEET THE GAFFERS

United's two first teams are managed by head coaches renowned as two of the best around. Let's get to know them…
▼▼▼

ERIK TEN HAG

MEN'S FIRST TEAM MANAGER

After his arrival from Ajax in the summer of 2022, Erik ten Hag quickly established himself as a boss with a long-term plan. Top-class new signings helped develop the type of squad he wanted, and the Dutchman's tactical skill and high standards soon had an impact, leading to Erik to win a major honour in his first season at the club. The 2022/23 Carabao Cup was the Reds' first trophy in six years, but Ten Hag's seventh in four years after hoovering up six trophies with Ajax.

"As we say in Brazil, he's the type of coach who will never let the cord slacken," said veteran Brazilian midfielder Casemiro, who has worked with some of the modern game's greatest managers. "He always wants the most from his players, he always wants to work harder, always wants to see the player develop. He always wants to win and does everything to win. He's a very demanding coach, wanting perfection. We know it's difficult to achieve perfection in football; in life and in football, it's difficult to achieve perfection, but he's obsessed, obsessed with perfection, obsessed with winning, obsessive in everything. He's a top manager, a top coach with an incredible obsession to win."

In his playing days, Erik was an intelligent central defender who was always obsessed with tactics and seemed destined to become a coach from a young age. Spells with Go Ahead Eagles, Bayern Munich's reserves and FC Utrecht were followed by steps up to Ajax and United, and his first season in English football brought two cup finals and a return to the Champions League. As Ten Hag himself put it at the start of 2023/24: "Last year went quite well for us, but there is always room for improvement. We cannot afford to take a few steps in the right direction and then stand still – it is our intention to keep moving forward."

Let's go, gaffer!

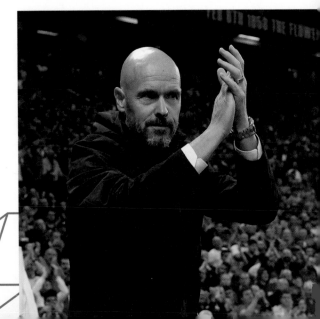

MARC SKINNER
WOMEN'S FIRST TEAM MANAGER

"We're just getting started." This was Marc Skinner's typically upbeat reaction to a best-ever season for the women's first team in 2022/23. A hugely uplifting presence around Carrington, Marc uses his positive attitude to inspire his squad going into every game, and was a major factor in the team reaching its first-ever cup final, posting a club record points tally and reaching the Champions League for the very first time. Having occupied various roles at his first club,

Birmingham City, Marc took on his first head coach role with the Blues in 2016 and he soon transformed the club's fortunes, taking them to the FA Cup final and overachieving in the Women's Super League. His work with Birmingham caught the eye of Orlando Pride in America and he worked stateside between 2019 and 2021 when United offered him the chance to replace former manager Casey Stoney.

It didn't take Skinner long to have an impact, winning two WSL manager of the month awards in his first season and three in his second, steadily overseeing improvements across the squad all the time. His team is dominant, entertaining and a regular contender for top honours, which he is determined to win for the Reds' fantastic fan base.

"There's such a great connection between these players and supporters," said Marc. "Everybody in our team and our staff wants to do well for our fans because we know how important they are for what we're trying to do. Everything we do is literally for them. Coming from a working-class background like I do, I appreciate the fact that they spend their hard-earned money to come and support us, and we try to put that into our performances. I know, deep down, that we're going to produce trophies for them. That's our ethos as a club and I hope we can give them that to present them with a symbol of how much we appreciate them. We will absolutely give everything for them."

We're in it together, boss!

THE TROPHY ROOM

Following United's Carabao Cup success in 2022/23, the Reds' collection of silverware has grown even further. So you know your history, here's every honour we've ever won…

20

LEAGUE TITLES

1908	1911	1952	1956
1957	1965	1967	1993
1994	1996	1997	1999
2000	2001	2003	2007
2008	2009	2011	2013

3

UEFA CHAMPIONS LEAGUE

1968 1999 2008

12

FA CUP

1909	1948	1963
1977	1983	1985
1990	1994	1996
1999	2004	2016

6

LEAGUE CUP

1992	2006
2009	2010
2017	2023

21

FA COMMUNITY SHIELD

1908	1911	1952	1956
1957	1965*	1967*	1977*
1983	1990*	1993	1994
1996	1997	2003	2007
2008	2010	2011	2013
2016			*Shared*

1

UEFA EUROPA LEAGUE

2017

1

UEFA SUPER CUP

1991

1

FIFA CLUB WORLD CUP

2008

1

INTERCONTINENTAL CUP

1999

1

UEFA CUP WINNERS' CUP

1991

2

FOOTBALL LEAGUE DIVISION TWO

1936 1975

1

WOMEN'S CHAMPIONSHIP

2019

11

FA YOUTH CUP

1953	1954	1955	1956
1957	1964	1992	1995
2003	2011	2022	

ANDRE
ONANA

GOALKEEPER

A player who is as comfortable with the ball at his feet as he is with the ball in his hands, Andre Onana represents a shift in how United are viewing the role of goalkeeper at Old Trafford. The Cameroon international has experienced life with Barcelona, Ajax and Internazionale, giving him a broad view of how the game can be played, and his confidence never wavers. A major presence both keeping out opponents and starting attacks, Andre is an entertaining, elite-level capture and is now reunited with former Ajax boss Erik ten Hag.

BORN – 2 APRIL 1996 >> NKOL NGOK, CAMEROON

ANDRE IN HIS OWN WORDS

"

I think the most important thing is to recognise the situation and that's what I do myself: read the situation, especially what the team needs in certain moments. When we play, depending on who we play, sometimes you have the possession and sometimes not, so from there you have to be smart and try to help the team. I look at myself as a modern goalkeeper, so I can adapt to any situation.

"

DID YOU KNOW?

As well as his existing links to United through Ten Hag, Andre has also been heavily involved with Reds legend Edwin van der Sar. The former Reds goalkeeper convinced Ajax to sign Onana, then mentored him during his time with the Amsterdam giants. Thanks, agent Edwin!

TEN HAG'S TAKE

"

We are happy with his physical presence and also with his personality. He is so keen on winning, he is so eager to win trophies, he will help the team and help the squad to get to higher levels.

"

LUCIA
GARCIA

FORWARD

A lively goal-getter who is in her peak years, Spain international Lucia Garcia arrived at United in the summer of 2022 and soon set about injecting energy into Marc Skinner's side. Having featured at the World Cup and European Championship with the Spanish national team, after winning the UEFA Under-17s and Under-19s Championships, Lucia also has a wealth of experience with her former side, Athletic Club. A star in the domestic league and Champions League, she enjoyed a strong first season in English football and will look to continue her non-stop approach as the Reds stalk the game's major honours.

LUCIA IN HER OWN WORDS

"
There's a great family atmosphere at the club, which is the exact environment in which I thrive. I will give everything I have on the field to make our fans proud, and hopefully score a few goals as well! This is a big club, I believe in this team, this is the reason I came here.
"

FOREVER
EVER

BORN – 14 JULY 1998 ⟫ BARAKALDO, SPAIN

DID YOU KNOW?

When Lucia was born, she was one of four quadruplets! She is also the only girl of the four, having been born at the same time as three brothers.

SKINNER SAYS

"
When I talk about the 'Red Devil' energy, it's Lucia – the way she moves, presses, invades the space behind the shoulder. The reason we signed her is because I think she can do that for 90 minutes.
"

MAN ON FIRE

In 2022/23, **Marcus Rashford** became the first United player in a decade to top **30 goals** in a single season. Here's how our no.10 did it…

STARTING AGAINST LIVERPOOL IN AUGUST AND FINISHING AGAINST CHELSEA IN MAY, MARCUS SCORED AT LEAST ONCE AGAINST 22 OF THE 28 TEAMS HE FACED

 ARSENAL ✓  CHARLTON ✓  LIVERPOOL ✓  REAL SOCIEDAD ✗

 ASTON VILLA ✓ CHELSEA ✓ MAN CITY ✓   SEVILLA ✗

 BARCELONA ✓   CRYSTAL PALACE ✓ NEWCASTLE ✓ SHERIFF ✓

 BOURNEMOUTH ✓   EVERTON ✓   FOREST ✓   SOUTHAMPTON ✗

 BRENTFORD ✓   FULHAM ✗   OMONIA ✓   TOTTENHAM ✓

 BRIGHTON ✗   LEEDS ✓   READING ✗   WEST HAM ✓

 BURNLEY ✓   LEICESTER ✓   REAL BETIS ✓   WOLVES ✓

HERE'S HOW HE SCORED

4 HEADER

7 LEFT FOOT

19 RIGHT FOOT

DID YOU KNOW?

In 22/23, **Marcus** became only the ninth youth team product to top-score in a season for United, and only the third – after **Mark Hughes** and **Paul Pogba** – in the Premier League era.

DID YOU KNOW?

Marcus is one of only 12 players to score more than 30 goals for United in a single season. **Denis Law** and **Ruud van Nistelrooy** both managed to do it three times, and Law's 46 goals in 1963/64 remains the all-time club record. Rashy, that's the target!

MAN ON FIRE
SHOOTING FOR THE TOP

Going into 2023/24, Marcus was on 123 United goals, almost halfway to Wayne Rooney's all-time club record of 253, set between 2004 and 2017. With time still on his side and a new, long-term contract signed, Rashy is aiming for the very top, which means – Wazza's record!

"Hopefully I will [break the record]," he said. "You never know what's going to happen, but I'm all about scoring goals and trying to make assists. There's a chance that it can happen. I've spoken to Wazza about it – he wants me to do it! He said it would be good for me to do it as I've grown up at the club. Hopefully I get the opportunity to try and make it happen."

Despite being United's top scorer in 2022/23 and starring at the top of the game since his late teens, Marcus is still determined to keep improving, and he's identified areas of his game he wants to keep working on.

"It's important to work on your strengths," he said. "You want to get your weaknesses as good as they can get, but they are more often than not always going to be a little bit behind your strengths. Mine are my left foot and heading – I always want to work on them. My heading is getting better, but I feel like I should score more because I out-jump most people. If I'm in the position in the right areas in the box, I should be getting more headed goals a season – I feel like I can do that, and I'll be pushing to do that.

"For me, my left foot is just about confidence and when I'm confident, I'll score with it. When I'm not confident, it just never goes right on my left foot. If I'm feeling confident, strong, fit and healthy, if I get an opportunity on my left, I've got a good chance of scoring as long as I'm in the right areas. My striker coach [Benni McCarthy] always gives me information on getting in across the front post, or on the shoulders of the defenders and stuff like that. I think there's always elements I can add to my game."

That's exactly the kind of attitude required to make it to the top. Keep going, Rashy!

RASHY THE CENTURION

During 2022/23, **Marcus** became part of a small group of players to pass 100 goals for United. Here's where he stands in our all-time scoring charts…

UNITED'S ALL-TIME TOP SCORERS
(Pre-2023/24 season)

1. WAYNE ROONEY	253 GOALS IN 559 GAMES	(0.453 goals per game)
2. SIR BOBBY CHARLTON	249 GOALS IN 758 GAMES	(0.328 goals per game)
3. DENIS LAW	237 GOALS IN 404 GAMES	(0.587 goals per game)
4. JACK ROWLEY	211 GOALS IN 424 GAMES	(0.498 goals per game)
=5. DENNIS VIOLLET	179 GOALS IN 293 GAMES	(0.611 goals per game)
=5. GEORGE BEST	179 GOALS IN 470 GAMES	(0.381 goals per game)
=7. JOE SPENCE	168 GOALS IN 510 GAMES	(0.329 goals per game)
=7. RYAN GIGGS	168 GOALS IN 963 GAMES	(0.174 goals per game)
9. MARK HUGHES	163 GOALS IN 467 GAMES	(0.349 goals per game)
10. PAUL SCHOLES	155 GOALS IN 718 GAMES	(0.216 goals per game)
11. RUUD VAN NISTELROOY	150 GOALS IN 219 GAMES	(0.685 goals per game)
12. STAN PEARSON	148 GOALS IN 343 GAMES	(0.431 goals per game)
=13. DAVID HERD	145 GOALS IN 265 GAMES	(0.547 goals per game)
=13. CRISTIANO RONALDO	145 GOALS IN 346 GAMES	(0.419 goals per game)
15. TOMMY TAYLOR	131 GOALS IN 191 GAMES	(0.686 goals per game)
16. BRIAN MCCLAIR	127 GOALS IN 471 GAMES	(0.270 goals per game)
17. OLE GUNNAR SOLSKJAER	126 GOALS IN 366 GAMES	(0.344 goals per game)
18. MARCUS RASHFORD	**123 GOALS IN 359 GAMES**	(0.343 goals per game)
19. ANDY COLE	121 GOALS IN 275 GAMES	(0.44 goals per game)
20. SANDY TURNBULL	101 GOALS IN 247 GAMES	(0.409 goals per game)
=21. JOE CASSIDY	100 GOALS IN 174 GAMES	(0.575 goals per game)
=21. GEORGE WALL	100 GOALS IN 319 GAMES	(0.313 goals per game)

LISANDRO MARTINEZ

DEFENDER

Few players have become such instant fans' favourites as Lisandro Martinez. The Argentinian defender enjoyed an unforgettable debut season at Old Trafford after his arrival from Ajax, establishing himself as one of the best centre-backs around with his ball-playing brilliance and tough tackling. Throw in a mid-season World Cup win with Argentina and the Reds' Carabao Cup triumph, and Licha's first season in English football was a dream come true. Having set the bar high from day one, Martinez is now all about maintaining those standards at Old Trafford for years to come.

BORN: 18 JANUARY 1998 >>> GUALEGUAY, ARGENTINA

LICHA IN HIS OWN WORDS

"

There's something in me that I was born with, which is probably my mentality. Life itself is tough, you're always faced with tough times and that's where you need to show your mental strength. I come from a family in which we didn't have everything. I'm very proud of everything I've gone through and it's that strength I have today.

"

DID YOU KNOW?

When he was 13, Licha considered giving up on football. His father, a bricklayer, told him he had to try a day's work with him, so he could see what life would be like without football, but Licha overslept and was late! That day made him realise that football was his destiny, thankfully!

"

TEN HAG'S TAKE

Licha is a warrior. He has a fighting spirit, but he's also very skilful and can deal with the ball.

"

LE TISSIER

BORN–18 APRIL 2002 ⟫ **GUERNSEY, UNITED KINGDOM**

DEFENDER

Signed from Brighton ahead of the 2022/23 campaign, the classy, cultured defender quickly slotted into Marc Skinner's starting XI and never looked back. Though she had to work extra hard to make it in professional football, regularly coming from the Channel Islands over to mainland Britain, Maya's huge talent was her passport to success, and she broke into Brighton's first team at just 16. Having been called up to the senior England squad and named on the standby list for the Women's World Cup, Maya's story is clearly only just getting started.

MAYA IN HER OWN WORDS

"

It is really good to be a role model for girls and boys back in the Channel Islands because they don't get that many opportunities to show what they are about. For them to see that I can do it and they can do it too, it is good for them to have something to push towards and have someone to look up to.

"

DID YOU KNOW?

Maya currently holds the record for the most WSL appearances made as a teenager – proving that she's been a top-flight talent from her very early years!

SKINNER SAYS

"

Maya will be a key part of what we do moving forward. The best thing about her is that she takes everything in her stride. She has forward-playing ability and can strike the ball really well. Her passing range is excellent. Her maturity and concentration and all these things –

SQUAD GOALS

The 2023/24 campaign marks the 30th anniversary of the Premier League introducing squad numbers. Put on your stats hats – we're getting numerical…

UNITED'S 2023/24 PREMIER LEAGUE SQUAD

GOALKEEPERS

1	ALTAY BAYINDIR
22	TOM HEATON
24	ANDRE ONANA

DEFENDERS

2	VICTOR LINDELOF
5	HARRY MAGUIRE
6	LISANDRO MARTINEZ
12	TYRELL MALACIA
15	SERGIO REGUILON
19	RAPHAEL VARANE
20	DIOGO DALOT
23	LUKE SHAW
29	AARON WAN-BISSAKA
35	JONNY EVANS

MIDFIELDERS

4	SOFYAN AMRABAT
7	MASON MOUNT
8	BRUNO FERNANDES
14	CHRISTIAN ERIKSEN
16	AMAD
18	CASEMIRO
28	FACUNDO PELLISTRI
34	DONNY VAN DE BEEK
37	KOBBIE MAINOO
39	SCOTT MCTOMINAY
46	HANNIBAL

FORWARDS

9	ANTHONY MARTIAL
10	MARCUS RASHFORD
11	RASMUS HOJLUND
17	ALEJANDRO GARNACHO
21	ANTONY
25	JADON SANCHO
47	SHOLA SHORETIRE

In the very first season of the Premier League back in 1992/93, each team would wear numbers 1–11, with three substitutes sporting 12–14. Ahead of the 1993/94 season, however, the league decided to introduce squad numbers, where each player would be allocated the same set number for the entire campaign. Since then…

UNITED HAVE USED  **53** DIFFERENT NUMBERS FOR THE PLAYERS TO MAKE A PREMIER LEAGUE APPEARANCE AHEAD OF 2023/24…

The following numbers have all been worn at least once by United in the Premier League:

 1 TO **44** **46** TO **49** **51** **53** **56** **73** **74**

YORKE

PELLISTRI

SHIRTS **19** AND **28** HAVE BEEN WORN BY THE HIGHEST NUMBER OF DIFFERENT PLAYERS - EACH HAS HAD 12!

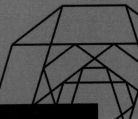

THE REDS' FIRST GOAL IN A PL SQUAD NUMBER WAS SCORED BY RYAN GIGGS, WEARING

NO.11,

IN A 2-0 WIN AT NORWICH CITY IN AUGUST 1993…

Giggsy also went on to enjoy easily the longest association with a single number, donning the no.11 shirt for 21 successive seasons before his retirement in 2014!

While Giggs stuck with just one number, his former team-mate **David Beckham** was less settled.

BECKS HOLDS THE CLUB RECORD OF BEING THE ONLY PLAYER TO WEAR FOUR DIFFERENT SQUAD NUMBERS IN PREMIER LEAGUE ACTION, SPORTING **28, 24** AND **10** BEFORE TAKING THE FAMOUS **NO. 7.**

 28
 24
 10
 7

BECKHAM

Six other players come close to Beckham's record, having sported three different squad numbers competitively.
Wes Brown, David May, Gary Neville, Phil Neville, Marcus Rashford and **Paul Scholes** all wore a trio of different shirts during their Reds' careers…

BROWN

MAY

G.NEVILLE

P.NEVILLE

RASHFORD

SCHOLES

19

SQUAD GOALS

22 7 9

SCHOLES

RONALDO

MARTIAL

SCHOLESY IS ALSO PART OF ANOTHER SELECT BAND: HE'S ONE OF JUST THREE PLAYERS TO WEAR THE SAME NUMBER (22) IN TWO SEPARATE SPELLS, ALONGSIDE CRISTIANO RONALDO (7) AND ANTHONY MARTIAL (9).

While numbers are supposed to be set for the season, three have been worn by two different players in the same campaign:

NANI

BLIND

FERNANDES

YOUNG

CAVANI

RONALDO

17 WAS WORN BY NANI IN THE OPENING GAME OF 2014/15, BUT AFTER HIS DEPARTURE NEW SIGNING DALEY BLIND TOOK OVER THE NUMBER.

FIVE SEASONS LATER, IN 2019/20, THE SAME HAPPENED WHEN BRUNO FERNANDES TOOK THE NO.18 SHIRT VACATED BY ASHLEY YOUNG.

IN 2021/22, EDINSON CAVANI STARTED WITH NO.7 BUT HANDED IT TO CRISTIANO RONALDO AFTER THE PORTUGUESE'S RETURN.

Sometimes, players do step aside and hand over their squad numbers to team-mates, often new signings. **Brian McClair** was the first, allowing **Andy Cole** to have his no.9 shirt, which **Zlatan Ibrahimovic** also did for **Romelu Lukaku** in 2017.

McCLAIR

COLE

IBRAHIMOVIC

LUKAKU

David May deferred #4 to **Juan Sebastian Veron** in 2001, it was **Fabio da Silva's** selflessness which gave **Robin van Persie** his famous 20 jersey, while **Edinson Cavani** graciously gave **Cristiano** back his no.7 shirt when the Portuguese returned for a second stint at the club in 2021.

MAY

VERON

FABIO

VAN PERSIE

CAVANI

RONALDO

Players have also requested number changes. **Luke Shaw** wore **no.3** when he first moved to Old Trafford, but after one season switched to **23**, which he had worn since breaking into senior football at Southampton. **Antonio Valencia**, who started his Reds career in **no.25**, felt he suffered from misfortune for a season after moving to the famous **no.7** shirt, so he duly changed back.

SHAW

VALENCIA

Defender **John O'Kane** has the unique honour of wearing a different squad number in all of his Premier League outings, debuting as **no.30** in 1995 and playing his second and final league game for the Reds as **no.24** in 1996.

O'KANE

OUR BIGGEST SQUAD NUMBERS

SHORETIRE

The highest number worn by a Red in the Premier League is **74**, which **Shola Shoretire** wore for his debut against Newcastle United in February 2021…

ELANGA

Three months later, in May 2021, Anthony Elanga – sporting 56 – headed home the opening goal against Wolves to register the highest number worn by a Premier League goalscorer for the Reds.

MAINOO

Kobbie Mainoo, wearing 73, became the most recent addition to the list when making his top flight debut against Leicester City in February 2023.

IF YOU PLAYED FOR UNITED, WHICH SQUAD NUMBER WOULD YOU WANT TO WEAR AND WHY?

Name:

Number:

*All stats correct ahead of the 2023/24 season.

CASEMIRO

18

MIDFIELDER

When Erik ten Hag looked for a new defensive midfielder to dictate his side's play, he chose one of the modern game's very best. Casemiro arrived from Real Madrid with 22 major honours already secured and it didn't take the Brazilian star long to continue the winning habit at Old Trafford, winning the Carabao Cup in his first season. A brilliant reader of the game, an imposing physical presence and a highly experienced, intelligent figure in United's approach, Case's influence is absolutely vital to the Reds' fortunes.

BORN - 23 FEBRUARY 1992 >>> SAO JOSE DOS CAMPOS, BRAZIL

CASE IN HIS OWN WORDS

"

When you've played in so many finals and lots of games and you have that experience, you try to pass on that experience, to instil calm in the team.

"

DID YOU KNOW?

While many of United's players enjoy gaming in their free time, Casemiro took it to the next level in 2020 by forming his own esports team called Case Esports!

TEN HAG'S TAKE

"

I call him the cement in the midfield. In and out of possession, he makes such a difference and he gives the team an extra edge and helps them dominate in the game.

"

AOIFE
MANNION

DEFENDER

If there was ever anything to underline the mental toughness of Reds centre-back Aoife Mannion, it is the manner in which she fought back from her second serious knee injury in February 2022. "I do feel a little bit different as a person, but also as a player," she said after fighting back to full fitness. "I find it easier now to see things as a longer-term process." Aoife's reward was a call-up to the full Irish side and a new contract with United, where her top-level experience in the WSL and Champions League make her a key member of the Reds' squad.

BORN - 24 SEPTEMBER 1995 >> SOLIHULL, ENGLAND

AOIFE IN HER OWN WORDS

"

I was just always drawn to football. I was really competitive, had that streak through me for that competitive edge, so the idea that every break-time and lunchtime I could be involved with something that I was going to be a winner or a loser, just really resonated with me.

"

DID YOU KNOW?

Irish international, super-competitive, childhood Celtic fan… is it any surprise at all that Aoife's hero when she was growing up was Reds and Republic of Ireland captain Roy Keane?

"

SKINNER SAYS

Aoife is a key part of our squad on and off the field, and consistently displays the values and leadership qualities required to play for Manchester United.

"

ON▶THE SPOT

It's one of the most nerve-shredding situations in football: 12 yards out, only the goalkeeper to beat. Gulp! These are five of United's greatest, most important penalties ever taken…

ERIC CANTONA

UNITED 4 CHELSEA 0 – 1994 FA CUP FINAL

After a goalless first half at Wembley, the Reds were bidding to overcome the Blues and add the FA Cup to the Premier League title. After Denis Irwin was spectacularly upended in the Chelsea box, star striker Eric Cantona was preparing to take his spot-kick when Blues skipper Dennis Wise challenged the Frenchman to a £100 bet. If Eric scored, he would win the money. If not, he would owe Wise the cash. Cantona accepted the bet, stroked home his penalty in nonchalant fashion – then did exactly the same again six minutes later when United won another penalty and Wise offered him another bet. The Reds went on to win 4-0, clinching the club's first-ever Double, and Eric had a £200 bonus!

RUUD VAN NISTELROOY

UNITED 2 ARSENAL 0 – QUIETENING THE INVINCIBLES

In 2003, Ruud van Nistelrooy hit the bar with a penalty against Arsenal which allowed the Gunners to go on a long unbeaten league run throughout the whole 2003/04 season. The following term, they arrived back at Old Trafford unbeaten in 49 league games. So, when United were awarded a second-half penalty, Ruud had his chance for revenge. The Dutchman steered home his effort and set off on wild, screaming celebrations at a delirious Stretford End!

CRISTIANO RONALDO

WIGAN 0 UNITED 2 – 2008 PREMIER LEAGUE TITLE CLINCHER

The state of play was clear going into the final day of the 2007/08 Premier League season: a win for United at Wigan would retain the title, regardless of how second-placed Chelsea fared in their game. Just over half-an-hour in, Wayne Rooney won a penalty and Cristiano Ronaldo, with 40 goals already scored during the season, stepped up and confidently slotted home the game's opening goal, sending goalkeeper Chris Kirkland the wrong way. When Ryan Giggs later added a second, the first part of the 2007/08 Double had been secured.

WAYNE ROONEY

BLACKBURN ROVERS 1 UNITED 1 — 2011 PREMIER LEAGUE TITLE CLINCHER

A point at Ewood Park would be enough for United to wrap up a 19th league crown and become the country's all-time leading title winners. In true Reds fashion, however, this straightforward mission wasn't achieved the easy way, with Rovers leading 1-0 from the 20th minute until the 73rd. Then, Chicharito was pulled down, a penalty was belatedly given and, after an agonising delay, Wayne Rooney thundered home an unstoppable effort from 12 yards. Title number 19, incoming.

MARCUS RASHFORD

PSG 1 UNITED 3 — 2019 CHAMPIONS LEAGUE HISTORY-MAKER

Ole Gunnar Solskjaer's start to life as United manager was the best ever, but history said even he couldn't inspire the Reds to overturn a 0-2 first leg home defeat at the home of PSG – something no team had ever done. Instead, despite missing several senior players, Romelu Lukaku's first-half double meant just one more goal was needed when, in stoppage time, Presnel Kimpembe was penalised for handball. Marcus Rashford showed his ice-cold nerve during a four-minute delay before smashing in an unforgettable winner. Astonishing.

UNITED'S TOP 10 ALL-TIME TOP PENALTY SCORERS

(Non-shootout)

RUUD VAN NISTELROOY   28
WAYNE ROONEY   27
BRUNO FERNANDES   25
CRISTIANO RONALDO   20
ERIC CANTONA   18
ALBERT QUIXALL   18
STEVE BRUCE   17
GERRY DALY   16
CHARLIE MITTEN   16
DENIS LAW   15

GOING INTO 2023/24, UNITED WERE ON 491 SUCCESSFUL PENALTY CONVERSIONS, NOT INCLUDING SHOOTOUTS. WHO WILL SCORE THE 500TH?

IN MARCH 1950, CHARLIE MITTEN BECAME THE ONLY PLAYER IN UNITED'S HISTORY TO SCORE A HAT-TRICK OF PENALTIES, NETTING FROM THE SPOT THREE TIMES IN THE REDS' 7-0 WIN OVER ASTON VILLA!

PICK YOUR SPOT

You've got a last-minute penalty at Old Trafford to win the game: where would you put it and how?

TOP STOPPERS!

► Not forgetting our glove-wearing penalty heroes either. Here are five crucial spot-kick saves from the Reds' keepers...

PETER SCHMEICHEL — 1999 FA CUP SEMI-FINAL VS ARSENAL

United's immortal 1999 Treble hung by a thread when Dennis Bergkamp stepped up in injury-time, but Big Pete plunged to his left, pawed away the Dutchman's kick and the Reds carried on to win the game before scooping all three major honours.

2007 TITLE CLINCHER — EDWIN VAN DER SAR

A draining title race with Chelsea could have gone to the wire without a crucial late penalty save in the Manchester derby, in which Edwin kicked away Darius Vassell's effort and preserved a 1-0 win at City. A day later, United were champions!

EDWIN VAN DER SAR — 2008 CHAMPIONS LEAGUE WINNER

Having survived a major scare when John Terry slipped and missed the chance to win it, Edwin was United's hero against Chelsea in Moscow. In sudden death, Nicolas Anelka saw his kick fended away by the big Dutchman and the Reds were Champions League winners for a third time!

2009 LEAGUE CUP WINNER — BEN FOSTER

A goalless draw with Tottenham took the 2009 League Cup final to penalties, and England international Ben made himself an instant hero by brilliantly stopping Jamie O'Hara's shot as the Reds went on to win 4-1 in the shootout.

DAVID DE GEA — 2016 FA CUP SEMI-FINAL

United led 1-0 at Wembley but were creaking under pressure when Everton won a penalty. Future Reds striker Romelu Lukaku stepped up, steered his effort towards the corner and watched on in horror as Dave plunged to his right and tipped it around the post. Heroic!

TRIVIA TIME

GOALKEEPER GARY BAILEY GOT HIS OWN HAT-TRICK, SAVING THREE SPOT-KICKS IN THE SAME GAME AGAINST IPSWICH TOWN IN 1980. SADLY, THE REDS STILL LOST 6-0!

UNITED GOALKEEPER ALEX STEPNEY SCORED TWICE FROM THE SPOT DURING LEAGUE GAMES, BAGGING AGAINST LEICESTER CITY AND EVERTON IN 1973 — THE LATTER WAS THE WINNER!

LEAH GALTON

WINGER

One of the original squad members ever since 2018's reformation of Manchester United Women, tricky winger Leah Galton embodies everything good about Marc Skinner's side. Off the pitch, she's a humble and popular squad member beloved by her team-mates and supporters, while on the field she's an absolute nightmare for opponents to defend against. Blessed with searing pace, dazzling trickery and – most importantly – heaps of end product, Leah is one of the toughest forwards to face in the WSL, and one of the Reds' most reliable attacking weapons, year after year.

▲▲▲

LEAH IN HER OWN WORDS

"

Three words to describe me would be: committed, definitely, to whatever I'm doing; positive – I'm a positive person and if someone is down, I'll put an arm around them to check if they are all right; and I'm going to say powerful for the last one, as everyone says I'm a powerful footballer.

"

DID YOU KNOW?

Having gone to America to study on a four-year scholarship, Leah's big break in football came when she was picked by Sky Blue FC in New Jersey during the 2016 NWSL college draft.

SKINNER SAYS

Leah Galton is one of the best wingers in the world, in my opinion. She is the most humble, hard-working, power athlete that has so much wonderful quality and control in what she does. I adore working with her, she makes us better every time she's in our team.

"

BORN – 24 MAY 1994 ≫ HARROGATE, ENGLAND

MASON ▲▲▲
MOUNT

THE RED DEVILS

7

MIDFIELDER

As he has repeatedly shown against United in the past, Mason Mount possesses energy, commitment and intelligence – plus stacks more qualities – in abundance. The England international midfielder was identified as a priority signing for Erik ten Hag in the summer of 2023, with the Dutchman viewing Mason as the perfect player to lead his side's pressing play in midfield. Signed from Chelsea, with whom he had first trained at just four years old, Mount is a middle man who will be key to the Reds' aggressive style under Ten Hag.

BORN - 10 JANUARY 1999 ⟩⟩ PORTSMOUTH, ENGLAND

MASON IN HIS OWN WORDS

I like to start off the press, to give the opposition something to think about and then to combine that with an attacking threat and rhythm of our own.

DID YOU KNOW?

Mason is one of just three players in United's squad to have previously won the Champions League, alongside Casemiro and Raphael Varane. He starred in Chelsea's 2020/21 final win over Manchester City, providing the assist for Kai Havertz's winning goal.

TEN HAG'S TAKE

He is a complete midfield player. We know his capabilities and he will absolutely increase the level of our team. He is going to contribute to our performance so much.

UNITED X CHAMPIONS LEAGUE

2023/24, the Reds returned to the UEFA Champions League. Here's all the stats and trivia from United's long and thrilling history with Europe's top competition…

FIVE QUICK FACTS

▼▼▼

UNITED WERE THE **FIRST-EVER ENGLISH CLUB TO ENTER THE EUROPEAN CUP** (THE ORIGINAL NAME FOR THE CHAMPIONS LEAGUE) BACK IN 1956.

THE REDS WERE ALSO THE **FIRST ENGLISH TEAM TO WIN THE COMPETITION,** BEATING BENFICA 4-1 AFTER EXTRA-TIME AT WEMBLEY STADIUM IN 1968.

OVERALL, UNITED HAVE **WON THE CHAMPIONS LEAGUE THREE TIMES,** ALSO WINNING 2-1 AGAINST BAYERN MUNICH IN 1999 AND BEATING CHELSEA ON PENALTIES AFTER A 1-1 DRAW IN 2008.

OUR 1999 VICTORY WAS THE MOST DRAMATIC CHAMPIONS LEAGUE FINAL ENDING. UNITED TRAILED 0-1 IN INJURY-TIME, BUT **TEDDY SHERINGHAM** AND **OLE GUNNAR SOLSKJAER** STRUCK TO SECURE AN UNBELIEVABLE WIN!

NO ENGLISH CLUB HAS PLAYED IN MORE **EUROPEAN CUP/CHAMPIONS LEAGUE FIXTURES THAN UNITED.**

TRIVA TIME

It took over 40 years for United to lose a home game in the competition! Between our first game in September 1956 and Fenerbahce's win at Old Trafford in October 1996 (courtesy of a late deflected goal) our home record was P26 W23 D3 L0!

OUR FULL EUROPEAN CUP / CHAMPIONS LEAGUE RECORD

P293 W160 D69 L64 F533 A284

BIGGEST WINS

UNITED 10 ANDERLECHT 0, EUROPEAN CUP, 26/09/1956
UNITED 7 WATERFORD 1, EUROPEAN CUP, 2/10/1968
UNITED 7 ROMA 1, CHAMPIONS LEAGUE, 10/4/2007
SHAMROCK ROVERS 0 UNITED 6, EUROPEAN CUP, 25/09/1957
UNITED 6 HJK HELSINKI 0, EUROPEAN CUP, 6/10/1965

MOST APPEARANCES

1. RYAN GIGGS — 151
2. PAUL SCHOLES — 130
3. GARY NEVILLE — 115
4. RIO FERDINAND — 89
5. WAYNE ROONEY — 85

MOST GOALS

GOALS (APPS)

1. RUUD VAN NISTELROOY — 38 (47)
2. WAYNE ROONEY — 30 (85)
3. RYAN GIGGS — 29 (151)
4. PAUL SCHOLES — 25 (130)
5. CRISTIANO RONALDO — 22 (62)

HAT-TRICKS OR MORE

Season	Player	V Opponent
1956/57	**DENNIS VIOLLET** (4)	V ANDERLECHT (H)
1956/57	**TOMMY TAYLOR** (3)	V ANDERLECHT (H)
1965/66	**JOHN CONNELLY** (3)	V HJK HELSINKI (H)
1965/66	**DAVID HERD** (3)	V ASK VORWARTS (H)
1968/69	**DENIS LAW** (3)	V WATERFORD (A)
1968/69	**DENIS LAW** (4)	V WATERFORD (H)
1997/98	**ANDY COLE** (3)	V FEYENOORD (A)
2000/01	**ANDY COLE** (3)	V ANDERLECHT (H)
2004/05	**WAYNE ROONEY** (3)	V FENERBAHCE (H)
2004/05	**RUUD VAN NISTELROOY** (4)	V SPARTA PRAGUE (H)
2009/10	**MICHAEL OWEN** (3)	V WOLFSBURG (A)
2013/14	**ROBIN VAN PERSIE** (3)	V OLYMPIAKOS (H)
2015/16	**WAYNE ROONEY** (3)	V CLUB BRUGGE (A)
2020/21	**MARCUS RASHFORD** (3)	V RB LEIPZIG (H)

COMPETITION WINNERS

There are three Champions League winners in the current Reds squad: Casemiro and Rapha Varane, who won five each during their time with Real Madrid, plus Mason Mount, who triumphed with Chelsea in 2021.

BOSSING IT

Sir Alex Ferguson took charge of the vast majority of United's games in the competition. In fact, more than double the rest of the Reds' managers combined!

SIR ALEX FERGUSON – P202 W110 D52 L40

SIR MATT BUSBY – P39 W25 D7 L7

JOSE MOURINHO – P14 W8 D2 L4

OLE GUNNAR SOLSKJAER – P14 W6 D1 L7

LOUIS VAN GAAL – P8 W4 D2 L2

DAVID MOYES – P10 W5 D3 L2

RALF RANGNICK – P3 W0 D2 L1

JIMMY MURPHY – P2 W1 D0 L1

MICHAEL CARRICK – P1 W1 D0 L0

OPPONENTS

United have faced teams from 28 different countries in the Champions League. Our history in the competition goes back so far that one country we visited – Yugoslavia – doesn't even exist anymore!

STADIUM TOURS

United have played Champions League ties at the biggest and most famous venues in European football:

CAMP NOU, BARCELONA ✓✓✓✓✓

WEMBLEY STADIUM, LONDON ✓✓

SANTIAGO BERNABEU, MADRID ✓✓✓✓✓

STADE DE FRANCE, PARIS ✓

WESTFALENSTADION, DORTMUND ✓

SAN SIRO, MILAN ✓✓✓✓✓✓✓

LUZHNIKI STADIUM, MOSCOW ✓✓

ALLIANZ ARENA, MUNICH ✓✓

STADIO OLIMPICO, ROME ✓✓✓

WANDA METROPOLITANO, MADRID ✓

MOST-FACED CLUBS

BAYERN MUNICH — 11 MEETINGS

AC MILAN, BARCELONA, BENFICA, JUVENTUS, REAL MADRID — 10 MEETINGS EACH

MOST-FACED NATIONS

- SPANISH — 48 GAMES
- ITALIAN — 34 GAMES
- GERMAN — 33 GAMES
- FRENCH — 24 GAMES
- PORTUGUESE — 23 GAMES

A STAGE FOR LEGENDS

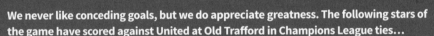

We never like conceding goals, but we do appreciate greatness. The following stars of the game have scored against United at Old Trafford in Champions League ties…

ROMARIO (BARCELONA)
ALESSANDRO DEL PIERO (JUVENTUS)
ZINEDINE ZIDANE (JUVENTUS)
GABRIEL BATISTUTA (FIORENTINA)
RAUL (REAL MADRID)
RONALDO (REAL MADRID)
KAKA (AC MILAN)
LUKA MODRIC (REAL MADRID)
CRISTIANO RONALDO (REAL MADRID)
KYLIAN MBAPPE (PSG)
NEYMAR JR (PSG)

BRUNO

FERNANDES

8

MIDFIELDER

Ever since his arrival at Old Trafford in 2020, Bruno Fernandes has been busy establishing himself as one of the Reds' finest-ever signings. The Portuguese international playmaker has provided an enormous goal threat from day one, whether scoring or creating countless chances for his United team-mates, and his stats are up there with any elite player in the modern game. Given his ability to lead by example and the fact that he hardly ever misses a game, it was a logical step when, in the summer of 2023, Erik ten Hag decided to make Bruno his club captain!

BORN - 8 SEPTEMBER 1994 >>> MAIA, PORTUGAL

BRUNO IN HIS OWN WORDS

"

try to focus on my game. I try o focus on whatever I can do nside the stadium, inside the pitch, because it's everything hat we can control ourselves. There is always noise around Manchester United, but I think if you keep doing the right things, if you keep the momentum, if you keep the results, the noise will always be less and less.

"

TEN HAG'S TAKE

I chose Bruno as captain because he is a great inspiration. He is the example, always wants to be a better football player, working very hard to give his maximum performance. So he is the mirror for many players and he is a good social connector. He is also very good in game understanding. For a manager, it's very good to have that integrated on the pitch.

"

DID YOU KNOW?

Bruno has a set routine every morning before he starts training at Carrington: he takes a ball into the indoor sports hall and tries to kick it through a basketball hoop. "Sometimes I have many attempts and don't get one, sometimes I get a small number. It depends on the day!"

ZELEM

MIDFIELDER

Another player who has been representing the Reds ever since 2018, skipper Katie Zelem is a childhood United fan who simply loves pulling on the shirt. A massive presence in the dressing room, Zel ensures that the collective is always working together and pulling in the same direction, while her abilities with the ball are an enormous part of the Reds' rhythm on the field. As well as her clever ball usage and tempo-setting, the set-piece wizard also has the incredible party trick of being able to score direct from corner kicks – which she did twice in one game against Leicester in 2022!

KATIE IN HER OWN WORDS

"

On the pitch, I would say my biggest achievement was captaining United for the first time. It was the Manchester derby at the Etihad in front of around 30,000 people. It was our first game in the FA Women's Super League, it was my first game as captain and my mum and dad were in the crowd and my Mum was crying, as usual!

"

BORN - 20 JANUARY 1996 >> **OLDHAM, ENGLAND**

FOREVER EVER

DID YOU KNOW?

As well as captaining United and playing for England, Zel is also on the PFA Players' Board, which assists with decision-making in English football. "I'm in a really privileged position with my club where my voice is heard," she said. "I can liaise with the staff to make change. I really wanted to do that on a bigger scale."

SKINNER SAYS

"

When I look at Katie Zelem, what people probably don't see is the way she gels and connects other players together. I'm proud to have her as my captain. She is a real leader and I've met many inspirational footballers in my time but she is up there for me. Katie can be a legend at this club.

"

TOM GRENNAN!

A promising footballer in his teens, **Tom Grennan** ultimately chose a career in music and the decision paid off spectacularly. Tom, whose latest album What Ifs & Maybes is out now, tells us about his love for the Reds, his outstanding United memories and his own footballing talents…

1

FIRSTLY TOM, WHY DO YOU SUPPORT UNITED?

I've got an Irish family, so they're all either Liverpool or United, and my cousin was quick to put me in a babygrow with a big United badge on it, so I think it just stuck from there! As I got older and watched more and more, United had some amazing years.

2

WHO WAS YOUR FIRST UNITED HERO?

When I started to know what football was and really appreciate the game, maybe around five or six, I just fell in love with **Paul Scholes**. I would always try to be him on the football pitch when I was playing with my mates. The way he could run a game stood out to me. He was just so cool on the ball, he never panicked and he could always move it about. I really like that kind of footballer and it was unbelievable how he played that role.

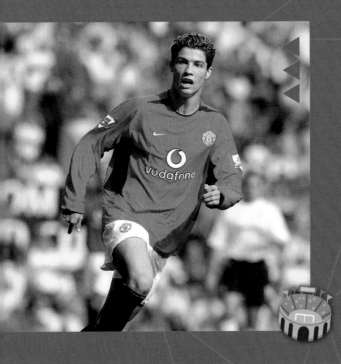

3

DO YOU REMEMBER THE FIRST GAME YOU WENT TO?

My dad took me to Old Trafford and we beat Bolton, it was 4-0 and it was **Cristiano Ronaldo**'s debut in 2003. I remember just being there, looking around the stadium and thinking: wow, I thought this place was a myth. I was just amazed that it was real and I was there!

4

WHAT'S YOUR FAVOURITE GAME YOU'VE ATTENDED?

I'd never, ever sat in the Stretford End until last season, when United played Barcelona. We beat them 2-1 and it was absolutely rocking in there. I think that would have to make it my favourite that I've been to. It was absolutely bouncing!

5

HOW ABOUT THE BEST UNITED GOAL YOU'VE SEEN?

It's got to be Wayne Rooney, obviously, against City. That overhead kick he sent into the top corner against them was just… wow. That's got to be the best goal I've seen any United player score.

6

YOU'RE A TALENTED PLAYER YOURSELF — WAS THAT OVERHEAD KICK SOMETHING YOU'RE CAPABLE OF ON A FOOTBALL PITCH?

(Laughs) Definitely not! I just love having a little bit of time on the ball and picking out a pass. That's how I play my football; I've never really been a goalscorer – although I did score in Soccer Aid at West Ham in 2022!

WHO'S YOUR FAVOURITE CURRENT UNITED PLAYER?

Casemiro, man. You can just tell that he's the boss there. Ever since he's come in, he just plays his football through the channels, he's strong on the ball, strong off the ball and he can change a game. That's the kind of player I love, people who can look at a pass before the ball's even at their feet. Football intellects, the kind who are always two steps ahead, they're my kind of player.

HOW WOULD YOU SUM UP OUR PROGRESS SO FAR UNDER ERIK TEN HAG?

It's definitely feeling good. He got silverware in his first year, got to another cup final and took us back to the Champions League. Again, he's just calm. You can tell that he's a calm, cool guy who can achieve a lot over time. There's more to come, more silverware and just as important is that it's enjoyable to watch under Erik. United are fun to watch, which is what you really want.

FINALLY TOM, WHAT'S THE BEST THING ABOUT BEING A RED?

For me, it's the history of the club. I love going back and watching old games to remind myself. That's the best part of loving United, being able to look back on so many achievements but also being able to look forward. There's a lot in the pipeline and I feel like there are exciting times ahead.

NIKITA PARRIS

22
FORWARD

Named the FWA Player of the Year in 2019, quicksilver striker Nikita Parris has been there, seen it and done it. From the age of 11, when she formed her own girls' football club in Liverpool, Nikita was driven to succeed in the game, and was playing for Everton's first team by the time was 16. She went on to represent Manchester City, Lyon and Arsenal before United pounced to sign her in 2022. A veteran England international with over 70 caps – plus a much-needed driving force for equality – she brings vital experience and know-how to the Reds' forward line.

BORN – 10 MARCH 1994 ❯❯ TOXTETH, ENGLAND

NIKITA IN HER OWN WORDS

" As an athlete, as a person who has a platform, it is so important that I use it and ensure that you help the next generation of people to help understand the cultural differences that we have. To be open too, and to also accept them because throughout my life I have met many different people and each person I have met, I have learned something new from. "

DID YOU KNOW?

Nikita's sister, Natasha Jonas, is a world star in boxing. Not only was Natasha the first British woman to compete in boxing at the Olympics, she's also a two-weight world champion!

SKINNER SAYS

" Signing Nikita was a no-brainer for me. She has this vibrant personality, she's aggressive on the field and wants to play hard, but off the field, she wants to have fun. I want that blend – I want my team to be the best and most united team, but when we get on the field, I want to fear nothing and she's another player that does that. "

MARCUS
RASHFORD

10

FORWARD

The emblem of United's attack, Marcus Rashford is our local hero who has raced up the club's appearances and goals chart ever since he burst onto the scene with a two-goal debut in 2016. A driving force for good in society, Marcus is also a top-class forward who enjoyed his finest goalscoring season in 2022/23. A new long-term contract in the summer of 2023 represented the ongoing commitment between the player and his boyhood club, and there's no telling just how far his talent can take both him and United.

FORWARD UNITED

BORN - 31 OCTOBER 1997 ▸▸ WYTHENSHAWE, ENGLAND

MARCUS IN HIS OWN WORDS

"

I joined Manchester United as a seven-year-old boy with a dream. That same passion, pride, and determination to succeed still drives me every time I have the honour of wearing the shirt. As a United fan all my life, I know the responsibility that comes with representing this badge and feel the highs and lows as much as anyone.

"

TEN HAG'S TAKE

"

From day one I was so excited to work with him. I saw his status and I knew already the impact he could have and his potential. Now he's bringing that potential to the pitch so I'm really happy with his development.

"

DID YOU KNOW?

Among his many tattoos, Marcus has three pictures of his previous family homes, plus all of his previous first-team shirt numbers for United. He explains: "They all mean something to me. My mum would shout at me if I got tattoos for no reason!"

DRESSING ROOM

TUNES!

Music has been a big part of matchdays for United players for decades. Going back to the 1950s, **brass bands** would celebrate winning trophies by playing popular songs as Sir Matt Busby's triumphant Reds lapped the field. Over time, post-match celebrations would be increasingly soundtracked by music from sound systems if the manager allowed it, but it wasn't until **Gary Neville's** installation as captain in 2006 that Sir Alex Ferguson agreed that his players could listen to music in the dressing room before each game.

Rio Ferdinand became unofficial dressing room DJ and would take suggestions, with every squad member providing two songs for a playlist. Over time, **Patrice Evra** and **Ashley Young** both took turns in the role, with France star Evra insisting: "I was the best. Rio and Ashley wouldn't agree with me just because they were jealous, but I didn't play songs I liked; I was making sure everyone in the dressing room was happy. You would hear some R&B, hip-hop, pop music, opera, Frank Sinatra, everything. Before the Champions League final in Moscow, I could see everybody was tense, so I played: 'Three Little Birds' by Bob Marley. It worked! I always made sure everyone was happy – this is why I was the best!"

Over in the women's first team dressing room, skipper **Katie Zelem** has overseen the tunes since United's formation in 2018, having performed the role with her previous club, Juventus. The England international has a job on her hands drowning out the singers in the squad, however, with **Ella Toone** particularly fond of belting out the karaoke classics.

"I've got a few favourites because I've got the voice of an angel," she laughs. "I like Islands in the Stream (by Dolly Parton and Kenny Rogers) and I pretend to be two people. Or The Man Who Can't Be Moved (by The Script) – I've done that before and it went down really well."

43

DRESSING ROOM TUNES!

> "I LOVE R&B, OLD-SCHOOL. THAT'S MY MAIN THING I'M LISTENING TO."
> **TYRELL MALACIA**

Over time, of course, careers end or move on and new players have to take on the responsibility of sorting out the pre-match tunes. Back in the men's team, **David de Gea** was renowned for playing heavy Spanish rock music in the early part of his United career. That met some opposition but, when **Bruno Fernandes** took on the role of DJ, he ensured that De Gea was always allowed to choose the last song before heading out for the goalkeepers' warm-up.

Now, while Bruno has become club captain, he has passed on the duties to other members of the squad. "I decided to not do it anymore," he laughed. "I don't want to waste my battery! Sometimes now it's **Diogo**, sometimes **Jadon**, it depends on the mood. Diogo goes more for the Spanish songs, Jadon does more of the English songs."

> "THE MUSIC I LISTEN TO IS HIP HOP AND R&B, ESPECIALLY WHEN I'M RELAXING; I LIKE TO LISTEN TO A BIT OF R&B AND CHILL ON THE SOFA. IN THE DRESSING ROOM WE LISTEN TO DRAKE, FUTURE, RODDY RICCH… IN GENERAL, WE LISTEN TO A LOT OF DRAKE, HIP-HOP AND R&B."
> **LUKE SHAW**

While speakers blare out tunes for everyone to listen to, some individuals do prefer to keep their headphones on and prepare individually. The majority of players listen to the team speaker, however, and while **Dalot** or **Sancho** are regulars at controlling the playlists, Marcus Rashford – who tends to request rap – revealed in 2023 that results ultimately decide who takes charge. "We have a rule that if somebody plays the music before the game and we lose, then they're off," said the United and England star. "They just have to go. If we're winning and we're listening to Portuguese music all the time, some of the English lads are sat there fuming!"

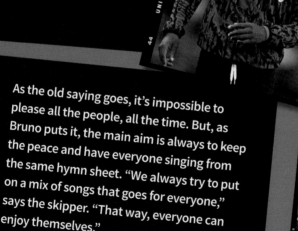

As the old saying goes, it's impossible to please all the people, all the time. But, as Bruno puts it, the main aim is always to keep the peace and have everyone singing from the same hymn sheet. "We always try to put on a mix of songs that goes for everyone," says the skipper. "That way, everyone can enjoy themselves."

"I LISTEN TO A LOT OF MUSIC, DIFFERENT KINDS OF MUSIC — HIP-HOP, INDIE-POP AND SWEDISH HIP-HOP. MY FRIEND SAMI, A SWEDISH ARTIST, ALSO RELEASED AN ALBUM WHICH I LISTEN TO BEFORE GAMES."
VICTOR LINDELOF

RASMUS HOJLUND

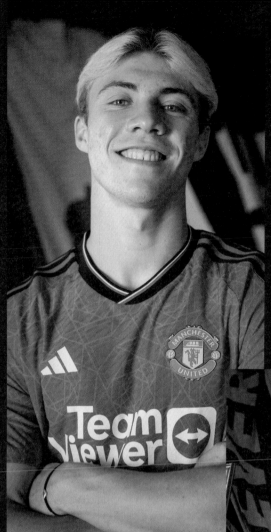

FORWARD

When Erik ten Hag was looking for a new centre forward to lead his attack, his attention was soon taken by Rasmus Hojlund. In the space of just three years, the tall Danish striker had moved up from FC Copenhagen to Sturm Graz and then on to Atalanta. Having also hit the international scene in style with Denmark, bagging a hat-trick in his first start, the 20-year-old convinced United's manager that he was the man to lead the Reds' attack. Lightning quick and extremely strong, Rasmus will be an exciting feature of United's forward line for years to come.

BORN – 4 FEBRUARY 2003 ≫ COPENHAGEN, DENMARK

RASMUS IN HIS OWN WORDS

"

I know the Premier League is the most competitive league in the world, and playing for Man United has always been my dream. So, this is two very important components which make me take this decision to come here. I want to bleed for this jersey, and I want to win some trophies, so that's why I came here. Of course, I'm 20 years old, so I have a lot still to learn, but I hope I can become a world-class striker as soon as possible.

"

DID YOU KNOW?

United's bid to sign Rasmus was helped by Reds midfielder Christian Eriksen, who told him all about the club while the pair were on international duty together with Denmark. Rasmus joked: "He called himself Agent Christian in the national team!"

TEN HAG'S TAKE

We chose him because he has the potential – the physicality, his speed, character, hungriness, determination for goals. It's absolutely the right fit, also his age fits very well in the profile, so we are very confident we found the right striker. He can make a real difference to the way we attack.

"

GEYSE

FORWARD

From her early years, when she would skip school to go and play beach football with her friends, Geyse always seemed destined to enjoy a special career. She left Brazil at an early age, joining Benfica before moving on to Madrid CFF and then Barcelona, where she immediately starred in a league, cup and Champions League Treble in 2022/23. Added to her success with Brazil, for whom she's a key player, and the forward arrived at United with incredible pedigree. With quick feet and an even quicker brain, she's a thrilling capture for the Reds' hopes of future success.

BORN – 27 MARCH 1998 ⟫ ALAGOAS, BRAZIL

GEYSE IN HER OWN WORDS

"

I started playing football with friends on the beach, then an opportunity came up through my PE teacher to go and play in a team. I accepted the offer and from then on, more opportunities came my way. I had to get up early and go to the capital to play football, but nowadays I think women's football is more valued than in the past. Every step that we take in women's football gives us joy that we're able to show we're capable of doing well.

"

DID YOU KNOW?

Geyse's inspiration for pursuing a career in football was her mother. "She is a warrior," said the forward. "My motivation was always to wake up early and travel 135 kilometres to training as it would be worth it to give a better life to my mother."

SKINNER SAYS

Geyse is a proven winner on the biggest stages. She has won both domestic and international honours and her winning mentality is an important addition to our team.

"

OUTSIDE INTERESTS

While United's players are all dedicated professionals, they do also have lives away from football. Here's how some of the Reds like to spend their time off the pitch…

CHARITABLE WORK

United's players are renowned for their brilliant work with Manchester United Foundation, the club's official charity, but they don't stop there. Not even close. The two first-team squads are tied up in all kinds of charitable ventures all over the world. Mason Mount, for example, supports the Make A Wish Foundation, while Bruno Fernandes and Victor Lindelof joined forces to raise money for UNICEF's Ukraine Appeal; Ella Toone teamed up with Tesco to back its Golden Grants programme to helps local communities; Christian Eriksen supports Danish children's charity Fodboldfonden and Luke Shaw raises awareness for Joseph's Goal, and there are countless more. Some have gone even further and started their own ventures, such as the Andre Onana Foundation, which provides medical care to under-18s in Cameroon, and the Marcus Rashford book club, which encourages children to get reading. Hopefully he recommends the Manchester United Annual!

FAMILY TIME

"You have moments sometimes when you have to disconnect from football because you have many tensions. Sometimes, you have to do other things. I think you have another life, outside of your club. I like to spend time with the people that I love. Sometimes, my girlfriend and I, we walk around with our dog to disconnect. Our dog is so funny."

LISANDRO MARTINEZ

SOCIAL MEDIA

Like the majority of the world, United's players are very active on social media's various channels, from Instagram to TikTok and all points in-between, the Reds are a constant online presence when the time allows. One of the most popular is national treasure Ella Toone, who has over 250,000 TikTok followers and her own YouTube channel. "Football is always first and I want to be remembered as a good footballer," she smiles, and adds: "If people connect with me away from football, that's OK too!"

ELLA TOONE

TRAVELLING

"My girlfriend and I like to travel on my days off. We've been up north. Grantley Hall [in Ripon] is probably our favourite place to go. We love to go to London by train as well."

DIOGO DALOT

OUTSIDE ▼▼▼ INTERESTS

WATCHING OTHER SPORTS

For the competitive types at United, watching other athletes do their job can be fascinating. Raphael Varane loves F1 motor racing, and was lucky enough to gain access to the Red Bull pit at the Silverstone Grand Prix in 2023. The French legend posted on his Insta feed: "What a sport!! 🤯 Amazing to see all the teamwork and excitement up close!!" There are countless sporting interests around the squad – Jadon Sancho loves American football and basketball, regularly watching NFL and NBA action, Scott McTominay is a big fan of golf, while Tyrell Malacia – who used to kickbox in his youth – loves fights and regularly watches UFC and boxing.

JUST CHILLING

"When I'm doing nothing, I just like to chill. Streaming series are my forte! Marcella is unbelievable, I like crime, true crime series. I liked Lupin, at first I refused to watch Squid Game because everyone was watching it but then I caved in."

KATIE ZELEM

EMBRACING ART

Many of United's players across the two first teams sport tattoos. Some might have one or two, while others are almost covered in them. For Victor Lindelof, body art is a serious business, with a story behind every piece on his body. "If you look at my tattoos, the first one I got was four birds, as I am one of four brothers, so that represents me and my brothers," he said. "One sleeve has a Greek theme because all of our names in the family are from Greece. I have Athena, so it's like a guardian and it also represents my mother looking over us and protecting us. We then just kept going with the Greek theme throughout the sleeve and a little bit of text for family because family is very important to me."

VICTOR LINDELOF

AND... EVEN MORE FOOTBALL!

"Every time I get the chance to see games, I'm always watching. If it's the Premier League, Championship, Portugal, Spain, France... I have friends everywhere! I will keep doing it because I think you can also improve your game by watching different styles of players and different styles of play in the teams. You can learn just by seeing football and understanding the movements and everything. You can enjoy at the same time and learn from that."

BRUNO FERNANDES

QUIZZES

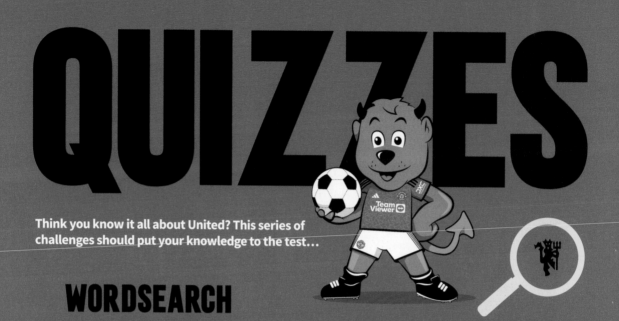

Think you know it all about United? This series of challenges should put your knowledge to the test…

WORDSEARCH

Can you find the surnames of United's starting XI in the 2023 Women's FA Cup final?

```
X  D  Q  O  G  Q  Z  P  A  T  G  W  T  L  J
W  R  Y  N  R  T  L  F  A  U  Q  T  C  J  N
S  Q  N  R  H  O  S  S  U  R  V  Y  M  Z  T
K  G  N  Y  M  H  F  X  S  N  R  I  Q  L  I
T  L  S  F  J  C  R  E  I  E  C  I  T  L  G
L  A  L  W  D  R  N  Z  C  R  M  S  S  D  B
S  D  Y  V  T  O  Z  A  X  Z  H  T  D  J  I
Q  D  P  M  O  C  Z  L  U  Z  L  W  K  I  B
D  L  E  T  I  S  S  I  E  R  E  J  R  M  E
S  G  N  W  E  N  C  U  S  N  E  L  P  Z  X
W  Z  A  D  D  F  U  A  S  L  P  Y  E  Z  H
C  N  B  L  U  N  D  E  L  L  G  Q  Y  M  W
I  Z  H  S  T  Z  Y  T  B  Q  Q  V  J  N  R
H  V  F  P  Z  O  A  E  E  A  R  P  S  D  J
W  K  M  O  U  B  N  H  Q  R  N  Q  X  I  P
```

EARPS   BATLLE   LE TISSIER   TURNER   BLUNDELL
ZELEM   LADD   PARRIS   TOONE   RUSSO   GALTON

ANSWERS ON PAGE 60

SPOT THE BALL

There are five footballs in this picture, but four have been digitally added by our designer. Can you identify which is the real ball?

WHO'S CELEBRATING?

We've covered the faces of 10 United goalscorers – but can you identify them by their celebrations, then match their name to the picture?

1

2

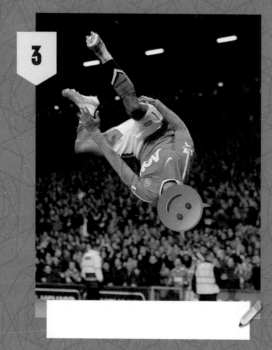

3

4

RASHFORD CAVANI ROONEY BECKHAM DALOT

LINGARD YORKE IBRAHIMOVIC DALOT NANI

5

6

7

8

9

10

ANSWERS ON PAGE 60

GOAL OR NO GOAL?

Take a look at these goalmouth action shots from 2022/23 – can you remember if the ball ended up in the net or not? Half did, half didn't. How's your memory?

1

TURNER VS ARSENAL

2

ANTONY VS NEWCASTLE

3

TOONE VS SPURS

4

FERNANDES VS FULHAM

GARCIA VS MAN CITY

GARNACHO VS WOLVES

RASHFORD VS BRENTFORD

GALTON VS BRIGHTON

ERIKSEN VS EVERTON

PARRIS VS ASTON VILLA

ANSWERS ON PAGE 60

SPOT THE DIFFERENCE

There are 10 differences between these two pictures of the MU Women first team in training – can you spot all of them?

A

B

ANSWERS ON PAGE 61

NAME THE NUMBER

The following trios have all worn the same Premier League squad number for United – can you work out which shirt number links the three players?

(HINT – Use our feature on page 18 for reference)

1 CANTONA, BECKHAM & RONALDO **NUMBER**

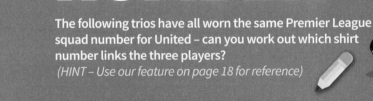

2 SCHMEICHEL, VAN DER SAR & DE GEA **NUMBER**

3 SCHOLES, FERNANDES & CASEMIRO **NUMBER**

4 IRWIN, EVRA & SHAW **NUMBER**

5 FALCAO, IBRAHIMOVIC & LUKAKU **NUMBER**

6 ROONEY, MATA & FERNANDES **NUMBER**

7 WELBECK, RASHFORD & VARANE **NUMBER**

8 SCHOLES, BECKHAM & FLETCHER **NUMBER**

9 KANCHELSKIS, HERNANDEZ & LINGARD **NUMBER**

10 V.NISTELROOY, ROONEY & RASHFORD **NUMBER**

ANSWERS ON PAGE 61

QUIZ >>> ANSWERS

It's time to see how well you know United...

WORDSEARCH

X	D	Q	O	G	Q	Z	P	A	T	G	W	T	L	J
W	R	Y	N	R	T	L	F	A	U	Q	T	C	J	N
S	Q	N	R	H	O	S	S	U	R	V	Y	M	Z	T
K	G	N	Y	M	H	F	X	S	N	R	I	Q	L	I
T	L	S	F	J	C	R	E	I	E	C	I	T	L	G
L	A	L	W	D	R	N	Z	C	R	M	S	S	D	B
S	D	Y	V	T	O	Z	A	X	Z	H	T	D	J	I
Q	D	P	M	O	C	Z	L	U	Z	L	W	K	I	B
D	L	E	T	I	S	S	I	E	R	E	J	R	M	E
S	G	N	W	E	N	C	U	S	N	E	L	P	Z	X
W	Z	A	D	D	F	U	A	S	L	P	Y	E	Z	H
C	N	B	L	U	N	D	E	L	L	G	Q	Y	M	W
I	Z	H	S	T	Z	Y	T	B	Q	Q	V	J	N	R
H	V	F	P	Z	O	A	E	E	A	R	P	S	D	J
W	K	M	O	U	B	N	H	Q	R	N	Q	X	I	P

GOAL OR NO GOAL?

1. GOAL
2. NO GOAL
3. NO GOAL
4. GOAL
5. GOAL
6. GOAL
7. NO GOAL
8. NO GOAL
9. NO GOAL
10. GOAL

WHO'S CELEBRATING?

1. DAVID BECKHAM
2. DWIGHT YORKE
3. NANI
4. ZLATAN IBRAHIMOVIC
5. BRUNO FERNANDES
6. WAYNE ROONEY
7. EDINSON CAVANI
8. DIOGO DALOT
9. JESSE LINGARD
10. MARCUS RASHFORD

SPOT THE BALL

5

SPOT THE DIFFERENCE

NAME THE NUMBER

1 CANTONA, BECKHAM & RONALDO NUMBER

 **7**

2 SCHMEICHEL, VAN DER SAR & DE GEA NUMBER

 **1**

3 SCHOLES, FERNANDES & CASEMIRO NUMBER

 **18**

4 IRWIN, EVRA & SHAW NUMBER

 **3**

5 FALCAO, IBRAHIMOVIC & LUKAKU NUMBER

 **9**

6 ROONEY, MATA & FERNANDES NUMBER

 **8**

7 WELBECK, RASHFORD & VARANE NUMBER

 **19**

8 SCHOLES, BECKHAM & FLETCHER NUMBER

 **24**

9 KANCHELSKIS, HERNANDEZ & LINGARD NUMBER

 **14**

10 V.NISTELROOY, ROONEY & RASHFORD NUMBER

 **10**

COMPETITION TIME!

One very lucky reader will win a 2023/24
United shirt signed by first team members.

To be in with a chance of winning, just answer this simple question:

Mason Mount is the latest player to wear United's famous
no.7 shirt – but who was the first Reds player to have **no.7**
as his squad number back in the **1993/94 season**?

A. BECKHAM   B. CANTONA   C. SCHOLES

TO ENTER, JUST VISIT
MANUTD.COM/ANNUAL2024

Good luck!

Jessica

Fabulous Fairytales

Cinderella

Beauty and the Beast

Red Riding Hood

Sleeping Beauty

HH
HERMES HOUSE

Cinderella

*O*nce upon a time, there was a beautiful girl with long, golden hair and eyes as blue as the sky. She was very happy until the day her mother became ill and died. Her father married again, but he too soon died, and the girl was left with her stepmother and stepsisters.

The two stepsisters were ugly and jealous of the girl's beauty, so they dressed her in rags and made her work all day. She slept beside the cinders of the fire at night, so she was called Cinderella.

Find the special stickers that you can add to this picture.

One morning, Cinderella was serving breakfast to her stepmother and stepsisters when four large, white cards decorated with gold crowns were delivered.

"There's a grand ball at the palace and we're invited," one of the sisters announced.

"The king has decided that it's time for his son, the prince, to choose a bride," said their mother. "He's asked all the girls in the land to the ball, so that he may choose one to be his wife."

"How lovely!" said Cinderella. "Can I come too?"

"No, you certainly cannot!" snapped her stepmother. "Your clothes are in tatters and besides, you will be helping us to get ready."

Cinderella was very upset and she rushed to the kitchen in tears.

On the night of the ball, Cinderella was very busy indeed. There were clothes to iron, corsets to tighten, make-up to apply and bows to be tied. There was much to do.

Add some fun stickers to these pictures. See which ones you can find.

3

Finally, the stepmother and stepsisters were ready. But despite their fancy dresses, fine jewels, and make-up, they still looked plump and red-faced. And without a word of thanks to Cinderella, they piled into their carriage and sped off to the ball.

Cinderella walked slowly to the kitchen. She sat near the fire and wished with all her heart that she, too, could go to the ball.

Suddenly, a voice behind her said, "Don't cry, Cinderella. You can go to the ball tonight and I am here to help you."

Cinderella looked round and saw a little old lady with a round, smiling face. She was wearing a red cloak and in her hand was a sparkling wand.

"Who are you?" Cinderella asked in astonishment.

"I am your fairy godmother," the old lady replied.

There are lots of lovely stickers for these scenes. Where can they all go?

"How can I go to the ball wearing these rags?" Cinderella asked.

The fairy godmother tapped her on the shoulder. Cinderella's rags vanished and instead she was wearing a white, silk gown that glittered with diamonds.

Cinderella twirled round and round, and the silk swished and rustled. Her feet felt as light as air and when she looked down, she saw that her old, wooden shoes had gone. On her feet she now wore two beautiful glass slippers that twinkled in the firelight.

"Now you can go to the ball," said the fairy godmother.

"But there is no carriage to take me," said Cinderella.

The old lady looked around the kitchen and saw an enormous pumpkin. She picked it up and carried it into the garden.

Where can the stickers go in Cinderella's kitchen?

The fairy godmother tapped the pumpkin with her wand. Suddenly, it changed into a glass carriage that sparkled like ice. Six fieldmice were then transformed into six white horses, and two frogs were changed into two footmen. It was a dazzling scene.

"Now, off you go to the ball," said the fairy godmother. "But you must leave the palace before midnight. At the last stroke of twelve, your fine clothes will disappear and you will be back in your rags."

Cinderella promised to do as her fairy godmother said. Then she thanked her, with tears of happiness and gratitude in her eyes, and she climbed into the carriage.

Find the stickers that will complete the picture.

At the palace, the ballroom blazed with the light from hundreds of candles. When Cinderella appeared at the top of the staircase, everyone stopped dancing and stared at her, wondering who the beautiful, young stranger could be. The band stopped playing their music and the prince looked round to see what was happening.

"I think she must be a foreign princess," sniffed one of her stepsisters, never dreaming that it was Cinderella.

At once, the prince ran up the stairs, took Cinderella's hands in his, and asked her to dance. She accepted and the music began. As they danced around the ballroom, Cinderella felt that all her dreams had come true.

The prince and Cinderella danced together all evening. The prince was falling in love with this beautiful girl with eyes as blue as the sky.

When the music finally stopped, the prince bowed and asked Cinderella to be his princess. But before she could answer, the palace clock struck midnight. Remembering her promise, Cinderella broke away from the prince and rushed from the palace as fast as she could.

At the last stroke of midnight, her beautiful gown changed back into her old, grey dress, and there was a pumpkin where her shining carriage had been.

Don't forget that there are lots of stickers to be added to both pictures.

Meanwhile, the prince had found one of Cinderella's glass slippers on the palace steps. It sparkled in the moonlight. He held it up and said to everyone around him, "My princess is the owner of this tiny slipper. I will not rest until I have found her."

Moving from house to house throughout the kingdom, the prince's footmen made sure that every young lady tried on the slipper. When at last they came to Cinderella's house, the stepmother and two stepsisters cried as they tried to squeeze their big feet into the tiny slipper.

Add some fun stickers to these pictures.

"Is there no one else in the house?" asked one footman.

"Only Cinderella," snorted the stepmother. "But she's just a servant, and she certainly doesn't go to royal balls."

"Every girl must try the slipper," the other footman replied.

The sisters went into the kitchen where Cinderella was peeling a huge mound of potatoes, and they brought her to the footmen. She put on the slipper and to the stepsisters' horror, it fitted as if it were made for her. Cinderella then reached into her pocket and pulled out the other glass slipper. It matched perfectly.

"We have found our princess at last," said the footmen, bowing deeply before her.

The footmen wrapped a cloak around Cinderella and took her to the palace. The prince was waiting for her at the top of the palace steps. As she ran to him, doves flew beside her, holding up her cloak.

"At last I have found my princess," said the prince, "and I will not let you go this time."

Invitations were immediately prepared for the royal wedding. When an invitation arrived at Cinderella's home, the stepsisters and stepmother were so happy to be going to the wedding that they forgot their jealousy.

Have you found some stickers to decorate this happy scene?

On their wedding day, everyone said how lovely the prince and Cinderella looked.

"You're not going to disappear at midnight again, are you?" the prince asked her.

"Never," Cinderella replied. "I will always be here with you."

Add the stickers to this page.

Beauty and the Beast

*T*here was once a rich merchant who lived in a very grand house with his three daughters. They were all very pretty, but the youngest daughter was the prettiest. She was always smiling, and her smile was so lovely that she soon came to be known as Beauty.

Her sisters were lazy and vain, spending most of the day admiring themselves and their fine clothes in mirrors, but Beauty had better things to do. She would often visit poor people in the village, taking them gifts of food and clothing.

There are some special stickers for you to add to this picture.

One day at breakfast, a servant brought in a letter on a silver tray. When the girls' father read it he turned as white as a tablecloth.

"All my ships have been lost in a storm at sea. We are now as poor as church mice, so we must move to a small cottage and find what work we can."

"Work?" snapped the eldest sister in horror. The middle sister said nothing, but greedily piled strawberry jam on her bread. She was worried that she would not have anymore for a while.

"Don't worry, father," said Beauty, "we'll be all right as long as we're together."

Beauty was so good that she was soon cooking for everyone and cleaning their new home, since all the servants had gone. She worked from morning until night while her two sisters did nothing but complain bitterly.

Find some stickers for these pictures. Where can they go?

One day, a messenger rode to the cottage and told the merchant that one of his ships had been found undamaged and filled with goods.

"I must go down to the coast at once," said the merchant. "Now, what will I bring back for you, my daughters?"

"New dresses!" the two sisters cried with joy.

"What about you, Beauty?" asked her father. "You haven't asked for anything."

"I would like a rose," she said, "a beautiful, pink rose."

The merchant set off and was away for a very long time.

With his business finished, the merchant headed toward home. He had brought dresses for his two elder daughters, but he did not have a rose for Beauty. He was worried that he would not find one, as it was winter and snowing heavily.

Suddenly, he saw a bright, white castle gleaming in the distance. He thought he could ask for a little food and water and also see if anybody knew where he could find a beautiful, pink rose.

See which stickers you can find to make the snow scene more busy.

21

The merchant put his horse in the stables and knocked on the castle door. No one answered, so he pushed the door open and went in.

"Hello!" he called. But there was no reply. He went from room to room and did not see or hear anyone.

Suddenly, a huge feast appeared on the table in front of him. The merchant was so hungry that he could not resist eating. He thought that the food was the most delicious food he had ever tasted.

When he had finished, he wandered to the window to see if it had stopped snowing. To his astonishment, he saw that the snow had gone and in its place was a stunning garden in bloom.

"What a magical place!" he said to himself.

The merchant went into the garden to pick the nicest rose he could find, when suddenly he heard a loud roar. When he looked up he saw a beast that was so horrible, the merchant almost fainted.

"So this is the thanks I get!" roared the beast. "I give you shelter from the storm, I feed you and then you steal my roses, the things I love most. For that you must die."

"I...I only wanted one rose as a present for my daughter, Beauty, who is the one that I love the most. Please spare my life."

"I will save your life on one condition. You must bring me the first thing that greets you when you get home."

"Oh, thank you so much," replied the merchant with relief, remembering how his dog always ran out to meet him.

There are lots of fun stickers to add to these pictures too.

The merchant got on his horse, and galloped away from the castle as fast as he could.

When the merchant arrived home, his heart sank when he saw Beauty rushing toward him, smiling her lovely smile.

He was holding the rose that he had promised and Beauty kissed him with joy for remembering. The other two sisters were too busy looking at their new clothes to thank their father.

"My dear daughter," he said to her. "I have paid a dreadful price for this rose." He then told her how he had promised to give the beast the first thing that greeted him.

"Don't worry, father," said Beauty. "I will go gladly. The beast can't be as bad as you say, and he may let me come home to visit."

The nex' ___ Beauty and her father set off for the castle.

When they arrived, they entered the castle and waited for the beast. Soon, they heard the beast's terrifying roar and saw his frightening face. The merchant and his daughter hugged each other in fear.

"So this is the Beauty for whom you plucked my lovely rose?" asked the beast.

"It is," said the merchant sadly.

"You must leave in the morning," said the beast to Beauty's father. "But rest assured, your daughter will be quite safe with me."

He welcomed Beauty to his castle by giving her a bunch of beautiful roses.

Don't forget to decorate both pictures with lots of special stickers.

25

Many weeks passed and Beauty lived safely in the castle. Although she missed her father terribly, and longed to go home, she found that the beast was very kind and gentle. Every evening she sat with him by the fire and they became friends.

Beauty had found a magical mirror. When she looked in it she saw, instead of her own reflection, that of other people. One day, much to Beauty's horror, she saw the reflection of her father lying in bed, looking very ill.

Beauty begged the beast to let her go home to nurse her father. He agreed, on condition that she return after one week.

"Thank you," she cried. "You really are so sweet and kind to me."

Can you find the stickers for these pictures?

Beauty arrived home just in time. Her father was very ill, but as soon as he saw his daughter he felt much better. She made him a soup using the special herbs that she had brought from the beast's garden, and the merchant felt his strength flooding back.

"Who does she think she is?" said one of her sisters crossly. "Fresh herbs at this time of year indeed, while I have to eat rotten old turnips!"

Beauty's sisters had not changed. They were still bitter and very ill-tempered.

Beauty lovingly cared for her father, while her sisters sat idly by. The week passed quickly and Beauty, still worried about her father's health, decided that the beast would not mind if she stayed a few more days.

Soon she decided she must return. When she arrived back at the castle she sat by the fire waiting, but the beast did not greet her. She searched the vast castle from cellar to attic, but she could not find her friend. In her desperation, Beauty searched the garden. And it was there that she found the beast lying on the ground.

Where can the stickers go in these pictures?

"He is dead," she thought. "I broke my promise and now I have killed him."

Beauty knelt beside the beast and held his rough, hairy hands, with their long claws. She began to cry.

When her tears fell upon his face, the beast opened his eyes and looked up at her.

"You broke your promise, Beauty. You stayed away too long and now I must die," he sighed.

"No," cried Beauty through her sobs. "What can I do to save you?"

"Will you marry me?" asked the beast.

"I will," replied Beauty at once.

There was a brilliant flash of light, the beast vanished, and in front of Beauty stood a handsome prince.

"Where is my beast?" she asked, looking around.

"Here he is," laughed the prince, holding out his arms. "A wicked witch turned me into a beast. Her spell could only be broken by a beautiful girl agreeing to marry me. You saw beneath my ugly disguise and have saved me."

On their wedding day, church bells rang out throughout the land. It was the most beautiful wedding that their guests had ever known. The couple lived happily ever after in the castle, and every day they went to the garden to see the roses that had brought them together.

Add the stickers to these pages to complete this enchanted story.

Red Riding Hood

There was once a little girl who lived on the edge of a forest with her parents. She was always outside playing games or helping with chores, so her mother made her a bright red cloak with a hood to keep her warm. The girl became known as Red Riding Hood.

One day her mother said to her, "Your grandmother is ill, so I want you to go and visit her. I have put some cakes and bread in this basket for you to take. But watch out for wolves in the forest as they are crafty and are not to be trusted."

There are some special stickers for you to add to this picture.

Red Riding Hood put the basket over her arm and set off. She had not gone very far when a hungry wolf, sneaking through the forest, stopped and sniffed the air.

"I smell fresh cakes," he said to himself. "Even better," the wolf thought gleefully, "I smell a lovely, fresh, tasty child."

He slunk silently through the trees until he saw Red Riding Hood.

"What a lovely day!" he said, smiling and licking his lips. "Where are you off to, my dear?"

He was so friendly that Red Riding Hood was not afraid.

"I'm off to visit my grandmother, who lives all alone in a cottage on the other side of the forest," she answered.

The wolf was delighted. Perhaps he could have a two-course meal!

Find some fun stickers to go in the picture.

"Well, have a lovely time," said the wolf, grinning hungrily, "Goodbye and good luck."

The wolf disappeared into the trees and set off at a pace to find grandmother's cottage. Eventually, he found it and went up to the front door and knocked loudly.

"Who's there?" a sweet old lady's voice cried from inside. "Do come in and say hello!"

The wolf pushed open the door. As the grandmother looked up in surprise, the wolf quickly gobbled her all up before she could say a word. He then put on one of her little bonnets and wrapped himself in her blanket. He curled up in grandmother's bed and eagerly awaited Red Riding Hood.

There are stickers for this picture and for grandmother's cottage too.

Meanwhile, Red Riding Hood had nearly reached the cottage. As she
wandered along she thought how friendly the wolf had been, and
she was very glad that she had spoken to him. As an extra gift for
her grandmother, Red Riding Hood picked a bunch of flowers.

At the cottage, she knocked on the door.

"Come in," said a croaky old voice from inside.

Red Riding Hood pushed open the door and stepped inside.

"Hello grandmother!" said Red Riding Hood. "How are you feeling?"

"Well, I'm not very well at all," answered the wolf in a gruff voice.

"Your voice sounds so strange," she replied. "You really must be very ill. Let me sit by you and show you the things I have brought."

"Why, yes! Come and sit close to me," said the wolf.

Which stickers can you find to decorate the room?

Red Riding Hood pulled up a chair next to the bed and sat down. The wolf's face was just peeping over the edge of the blanket.

"You don't look like yourself at all today, grandmother," she said. "In fact, how big and shiny your eyes seem!"

"All the better to see you with, my dear," croaked the wolf, licking his lips.

"But how long and pointed your nose looks all of a sudden."

"All the better to smell you with," snarled the wolf softly.

"And your ears," Red Riding Hood said, "they seem to be sticking straight up out of your bonnet."

"All the better to hear you with," smiled the wolf, who was beginning to feel quite hungry again.

"As for your teeth," she said, backing away slightly, "they're absolutely enormous!"

At that moment the wolf jumped out from under the blanket and roared loudly, "All the better to eat you with!"

But before Red Riding Hood had the chance to say another word or to run away, the wolf swallowed her down in one huge gulp!

There are some stickers to make the pictures even more exciting.

The wolf's tummy was very full and his two large meals had made him sleepy. Soon he was fast asleep and snoring loudly.

A woodcutter, who happened to be passing by the cottage, stopped when he heard the loud noises.

"That's strange," he said to himself, "I knew the old woman was ill but she must be getting worse to make such a din. I will pop in to see how she is."

As he pushed open the door he saw the wolf, with his head lolling against a pillow, his mouth wide open, and snoring loudly.

Place the stickers where you think they should go in this picture.

The woodcutter knew all about crafty wolves, and he realized what had happened to the woman. He rushed toward the sleeping wolf and slit open the wolf's stomach with his axe.

Red Riding Hood jumped out, followed by her grandmother. They both looked very surprised at what had happened.

44

"Oh, thank you," they both cried, "it was horrible in there, so dark and damp. What a bad wolf he was."

The woodcutter took the wolf and threw him into the lake at the end of grandmother's garden.

"We won't be seeing him again," he said.

Add some more stickers to complete these pictures.

Back in the cottage, grandmother was boiling a kettle of water.
"Both of you must stay and have some tea and cake," she said.
They all talked and laughed as they enjoyed the delicious food, and
then the woodcutter walked Red Riding Hood safely home.

Add the stickers to these pictures to complete the story.

46

Sleeping Beauty

Many years ago, a king and queen lived in a magnificent castle. They were very happy together, but they had no children and this was their only sadness.

One day they discovered that they would soon have a baby and they cried tears of joy. When a lovely princess was born, they decided to have a huge feast to celebrate. They would invite friends and family, as well as the fairies to bless the princess with luck.

See what special stickers you can find for the king and the baby princess.

The preparations for the feast involved everyone in the castle. The cooks started cooking and the helpers started helping, so that soon there were mounds of chickens, hams and cakes ready. The only problem was that there were thirteen fairies in the kingdom and only twelve gold plates. The king solved the problem by not inviting the thirteenth fairy.

The feast began and everyone was very excited. Whoever saw the baby said that she was beautiful, and the twelve fairies came with many magical gifts. All was going well until suddenly the door to the banquet hall flew open.

Decorate the party scene with some fun stickers.

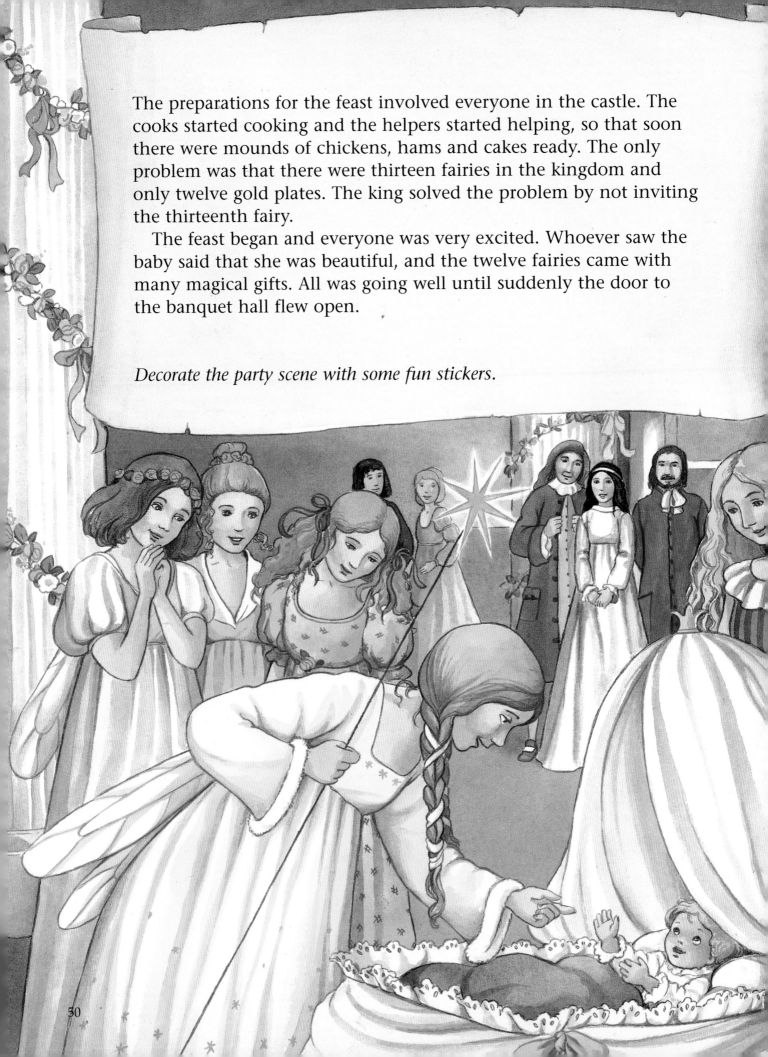

Into the room hobbled the fairy who had not been invited. She was old, dressed in a black cloak and her face was red with anger.

"So you didn't bother to ask me?" she cackled bitterly. "Well, I came anyway, and I have brought the princess a magic gift and a blessing."

The old fairy hobbled over to the cradle and pointed a long, bony finger at the baby.

"When you are sixteen," she cursed, "you will prick your finger on a spindle and you will fall down dead!"

Then she turned, and before anyone could speak, she was gone.

The guests were speechless with shock, and the queen burst into tears, hugging her husband for comfort.

One of the twelve fairies immediately stepped forward.

"I can't undo another fairy's spell," she said, "but I can help a little. The princess will prick her finger on a spindle, but instead of dying, she and everyone in the castle will fall into a deep sleep that will last for a hundred years."

Find the stickers for the nasty fairy and those for the queen.

The king did everything he could in his power to make sure that the old fairy's spell would not happen. He made a law that spindles were to be banned from his kingdom. He ordered that they be thrown on a huge bonfire. Posters were stuck everywhere, warning that anyone found with a spindle would spend the rest of their days locked in the deepest, darkest dungeon in the king's castle.

The princess grew up to be beautiful, happy and good. The king and queen tried to forget about the terrible curse upon her.

On the day of the princess's sixteenth birthday, everyone except the princess was busy preparing for a party. No one could spare the time to keep the princess company.

There are stickers to add to these pictures. Have you found them?

The princess roamed from room to room, her silk slippers disturbing dust that had settled years ago. Suddenly, she came to a narrow, winding staircase that she had never seen before.

"I wonder where it leads?" she thought.

She climbed the stairs, and cobwebs brushed against her golden hair.

At the top of the stairs was a thick, wooden door, and from behind it came singing and a strange, whirring noise.

The princess opened the door and went in. A little old woman was sitting at a spinning wheel. Her spindle moved as fast as the wind, its point catching the light from the window.

Which stickers will fit in these pictures?